SEATTLE, WASHINGTON

A PHOTOGRAPHIC PORTRAIT

PHOTOGRAPHS BY

Roger L. Johnson

First published in the United States
of America by:

Twin Lights Publishers, Inc.
8 Hale Street
Rockport, Massachusetts 01966
Telephone: (978) 546-7398
http://www.twinlightspub.com

ISBN: 1-885435-63-0
ISBN: 978-1-885435-63-7

10 9 8 7 6 5 4 3 2 1

Editorial researched and written by:
Francesca Yates and Duncan Yates

Book design by
SYP Design & Production, Inc.
http://www.sypdesign.com

Printed in China

Sunset on Puget Sound

Seattle is blessed with a spectacular
setting on Puget Sound. Due west
across the Sound, the jagged, snow-
capped Olympic Mountains rise
over 8,000 feet and protect Seattle
from the harsh weather that moves
in from the northern Pacific Ocean.

Introduction

Much like a large shield protecting an ancient warrior in battle, the Olympic Peninsula and its mountain range protect Seattle from the strong winds and rains that constantly move across the Pacific. Safely nestled along the evergreen shores of Elliott Bay in Puget Sound, Seattle enjoys a surprisingly temperate year-round climate, even though Canada is just 113 miles away.

Today Seattle has re-invented itself as a major, world player. The unprecedented success of native son Bill Gates' Microsoft Corporation has helped transform this once blue-collar city into a pros-

perous, hi-tech hub of software, Internet, medical and biotech industries. The port of Seattle is one of the most important areas of international marine commerce in the country.

This scenic and cultured Northwest city, amidst postcard views of mountain ranges and waterways, is a very special place.

Whether you plan to move or vacation here, or just celebrate the fact that this is your home, we invite you to enjoy our photographic portrait of this great Northwestern city.

**Hurricane Ridge,
Olympic Peninsula** *(above)*

A slow, zigzag drive up to Hurricane Ridge rewards visitors with a "top of the world" view of the jagged peaks of the Olympic Mountains. A heavy, annual snowfall adds to the power of the glaciers that relentlessly carve this alpine landscape.

Snoqualmie Falls *(above and opposite)*

The scenic village of Snoqualmie is nestled in the foothills of the beautiful, fog-laced Cascade Mountains, known as the "American Alps". The area is best known for Snoqualmie Falls, one of the most popular attractions in the state.

The 270-ft. deluge of this spectacular waterfall is one hundred feet higher than Niagara Falls. Next door, the posh Salish Lodge and Spa, a world-class resort, offers the perfect retreat in this stunning setting, just 30 miles east of Seattle.

Vashon Island and Mount Rainier

One of several wooded islands on
Puget Sound, with magnificent,
360-degree views of Seattle and
Mt. Rainier, Vashon is home to a
dynamic mix of telecommuting
professionals, farmers and cottage
industry entrepreneurs.

Maury Island *(top)*

Once separate from Vashon Island, Maury Island is now connected via a narrow strip of land wide enough for a roadway. Visitors can sightsee on Vashon and then visit the historic Point Robinson Lighthouse on Maury Island.

Carnation Farms *(bottom)*

Carnation Farms was the original site of the Carnation Dairy Company. The small, farming town that grew nearby was named after the company's founder. The historic farm is now the worldwide training center for the Nestle Company.

Vashon Island Golf & Country Club

(above)

A "to do" list for Vashon Island
would definitely include: play golf,
bike on country roads, visit working
farms, horseback ride, go to the
beach, visit an historic lighthouse,
enjoy the farmers' market, and go
boating, fishing, and swimming.

View from a Bi-Plane

(opposite)

Bridges span lakes, rivers, and waterways, connecting Seattle's burgeon-
ing suburbs and surrounding com-
munities with the city's vibrant
downtown. In the distance, Mt.
Rainier beckons.

Fireboat on Lake Union *(top)*

Lake Union has its own fireboat for quick response on freshwater. The 123-ft Alki, is a familiar sight on this downtown lake and pumps out over 16,000 gallons of water per minute and 1,000 gallons of foam.

Rowing on Lake Union *(bottom)*

The calm, flat waters of Lake Union give novice boaters a comfortable way to hone rowing and kayaking skills, while enjoying the scenery around this popular lake, located in the heart of the city.

Lake Union Neighborhood

Nestled on the hills around this busy, urban lake are high-end homes, condos, and cutting-edge biotech businesses. The brown, industrial structures behind the sailboats are Gas Works Park (page 29), once the site of a coal-to-gas refinery.

**Manresa Castle Hotel
Port Townsend** *(opposite, top)*

In the 1890's, when Port Townsend was a flourishing community with big dreams of being a terminus for the railroad, this 30-room castle was built by a local tycoon. The railroad never came, and today the castle is a unique and stately hotel.

Port Townsend Ferry Dock

(opposite, bottom)

The Washington State Ferry system is a vital part of life in Puget Sound, connecting islands with other islands and the mainland. The ferry service between Port Townsend and neighboring Whidbey Island carries 800,000 passengers yearly.

**Port Townsend Harbor,
Olympic Peninsula** *(above)*

Nicknamed "Victorian City" due to its large number of 19th century mansions, Port Townsend's charming, off-beat personality and picturesque harbor, attract tourists from all over the world.

Future Sailors, Port Townsend

A happy group of children learn
boating skills on a big, wooden boat
near shore. Across the bay, the snow-
capped peaks of the Olympic
Mountains sparkle under a clear,
blue sky.

Port Townsend and Olympic Mountains

Located on the northeast corner of the Olympic Peninsula, Port Townsend is the perfect departure point for whale-watching boat tours of the fabulous San Juan Islands. An Orca whale rising out of the water is guaranteed to give you chills!

Fort Worden State Park, Near Port Townsend *(above)*

Once important for the defense of Puget Sound cities, Fort Worden is now enjoyed for its stunning setting overlooking Puget Sound and Mt. Hood, its scenic trails and campgrounds, and a first-class business conference center.

Point Wilson Lighthouse, Fort Worden State Park *(opposite)*

This historic 1913 lighthouse is one of the most important navigational aids in the state, connecting Puget Sound and the Strait of Juan de Fuca. Mount Baker, an 11,800-ft glacier-covered mountain, looms in the background.

**Point Wilson Lighthouse,
Fort Worden State Park**

This historic 1913 lighthouse is one of the most important navigational aids in the state, connecting Puget Sound and the Strait of Juan de Fuca. Mount Baker, an 11,800-ft glacier-covered mountain, looms in the background.

Discovery Park Beach

Once an active military fort, Discovery Park is now one of Seattle's favorite urban getaways with miles of easy, walking trails along the beach and through the dense woods of the rolling hills above—all within the city limits.

Discovery Park *(top)*

The views from this waterside park are always captivating. To the south, the city skyline sparkles while snow-capped Mt. Baker shimmers in the distance. Late afternoons reward visitors with gloriously pink sunsets over the distant Olympic Mountains.

Hiram M. Chittenden Locks *(bottom)*

Built in 1911 by the U.S. Army Corp of Engineers, the Hiram Chittenden Locks provide a vital link between the salt waters of Puget Sound to the west and the fresh waters of Lakes Union and Washington to the east.

**Fort Worden State Park,
Olympic Peninsula**

Amidst a field of summer wildflow-
ers, this authentic Victorian house is
one of many outstanding Victorian
structures that show park visitors
what life was like a century ago at
this important, Puget Sound fort.

Scenic Olympic Peninsula Highway

Highway 101 is a truly "wonder-full" drive. This winding road loops around the peninsula and takes you from farm lands to rain forests, from Pacific Ocean beaches to forest-rimmed lakes, and from the Olympic Mountains to small towns with big personalities.

Sculpture at the Hiram M. Chittenden Locks *(opposite, top)*

"Salmon Waves" is a provocative, sculpture of seven stainless steel waves by artist Paul Sorey. It symbolizes the spilling of water over the dam that separates fresh and salt water at the locks.

Children Tour the Locks *(opposite, bottom)*

From August to November, tourists and school groups can go below to underwater viewing windows and witness salmon passing through the fish ladder on their annual spawning journey.

Kenmore Air Seaplane on Lake Union *(above)*

From its Lake Union terminal, Kenmore Air's seaplanes offer daily flights to the nearby San Juan Islands and the Canadian ports of Vancouver and the Gulf Islands. Take-offs and landings are always a thrilling sight.

**Houseboat Community on
Lake Union**

When Tom Hanks moved into a fabulous houseboat in "Sleepless in
Seattle," this charming community
became instantly famous. Once an
area where make-shift houses were
built on logs, the average houseboat
today has a six-figure price tag.

Evergreen Point Floating Bridge, Lake Washington

The longest floating bridge in the world at 7,578 feet, Evergreen Point is just one of the bridges that connect Seattle with the commuter cities on the eastern shores of Lake Washington. Prior to bridges, ferries carried commuters back and forth.

Gas Works Park, Lake Union

(opposite and top)

Only a great amount of creativity and persistence can transform an old, coal-to-gas refinery into an innovative, city park, without tearing down the original buildings. That's why Seattle's much-maligned and internationally acclaimed Gas Works Park is so delightful. The old boiler house is now a picnic shelter, and the former exhauster-compressor building is a children's play barn with a giant jungle gym of brightly colored pipes and machinery.

"Sundial" Sculpture, Gas Works Park *(bottom)*

Gas Works Park comes complete with its own 28-ft. sundial at the top of "Kite Hill," sculpted by artists Charles Greening and Kim Lazare. The park's scenic setting creates an ideal place for watching the lake's celebrated 4th of July fireworks.

Children's Museum, Seattle City Center *(above)*

Inside of child-size, interactive exhibits, kids ride a fire truck, slide down a glacier, visit bats in a cave, perform in a real play, explore world cultures, become a radio deejay, work in a flower shop, and serve their family at a Mexican restaurant.

Experience Music Project, Seattle Center *(opposite)*

Inside of this funky, cherry-red and steel building, designed by renowned architect Frank O. Gehry, is the first institution in the world devoted to exploring and celebrating the unique experience of music making.

Pike Place Public Market

(top and bottom)

A beloved Seattle landmark on the downtown waterfront, Pike Place, with its familiar sign and hundreds of shops and restaurants, attracts millions of people annually. Open-air stands greet visitors with locally grown, fresh flowers, fruits, nuts, vegetables, meats, poultry, seafood, jams, jellies and honey. Since 1907, the country's oldest, continuously run farmers' market has survived developers' wrecking balls several times.

Beware of Flying Fish!

(opposite)

When buying seafood here, vendors traditionally yell and throw it at you! From street level, shoppers walk down two more levels through a labyrinth of quaint shops selling Native American crafts, books, jewelry, magic tricks, and much, much more.

First Starbucks Coffee Shop

(top)

Once upon a time, there was only one Starbucks coffee shop in the world, and it was, and still is, located here at Pike Place Market. Seattle's reverent passion for a great cup of coffee has since spread to most corners of the world—even China!

Museum of History and Industry

(bottom)

This popular Seattle attraction is now the largest, private heritage organization in the state, attracting over 60,000 visitors annually. Its award-winning, provocative exhibits and programs bring 150 years of Pacific Northwest history to light.

Seattle Waterfront Trolley

Hop aboard this antique trolley and take a nostalgic ride along Seattle's downtown waterfront from Alaskan Way to the Chinatown International District. This special fleet of five vintage cars carries 400,000 passengers yearly.

Burke Museum of Natural History, University of Washington

Dinosaur bones, gems and crystals, plants and fungi, Native American arts and artifacts—these are just a few of the five million specimens in Burke's nationally ranked collections showcasing the natural history and cultures of the Pacific Rim.

Landscape Art, University of Washington

The Seattle campus is graced with an outstanding collection of outdoor sculptures that constantly provoke and involve pedestrians. The university offers a very popular "Sculpture and Public Art" class.

Suzzallo Library, University of Washington

This famous "cathedral of learning" features a spectacular 240-ft-long graduate reading room with vaulted ceilings and stained glass windows. The design was inspired by former university president Henry Suzzallo.

William H. Gates Hall, University of Washington

This $80-million law school is named for the father of Microsoft's Bill Gates, an alumnae and philanthropist. At night, the trapezoidal skylights of the library become campus lanterns as students burn the midnight oil below.

Ferry Arrives at Downtown Waterfront *(top)*

Ferries have always been a reliable and romantic way to travel around the Puget Sound area. Once aboard, commuters from Bainbridge, Vashon, Bremerton and other islands can enjoy a hot meal, a good book and beautiful views.

Sightseeing from the Ferry

(bottom)

Sparkling salt water, cityscapes, snow-capped mountains, and leaping Orca whales—it is no surprise that riding on a ferry is a great adventure. Ten ferry routes take tourists to nearby islands and the San Juan Islands further north.

Sightseeing Boats

Great adventures await you along
Seattle's waterfront. Sightseeing
boats will whisk you off on a grand
tour of Puget Sound's scenic islands
(complete with whale-watching),
and exotic ports-of-call in Victoria
and Vancouver BC.

Lake Washington Ship Canal *(top)*

This aerial view shows the canal as it winds its way from Lake Washington on the east to Seattle's Chittenden Locks. Once there, boats and ships are lowered through two locks to continue their journey into Puget Sound.

Seattle Ferry Terminal *(bottom)*

Massive, multi-deck ferries carry hundreds of cars below and thousands of passengers above. Over 26 million people come aboard every year to go to work, sightsee, or just to enjoy a sunny day or a magnificent northwest sunset.

Seattle from Elliott Bay

Across Puget Sound from Seattle, sandy Alki Beach provides an ideal vantage point for panoramic city, mountain, and water views. In the late afternoon, the beach is a favorite, romantic setting for watching golden sunsets.

Sunrise on Lake Union *(previous page)*

Lake Union, with its sweeping views of the city skyline and the mountains beyond, is an important link in the chain of waterways and locks that move boats and ships between Lake Washington to the east and Puget Sound and the Pacific Ocean to the west.

Seattle Public Library *(above)*

Walking around the city, you can't help but notice that reading is a passionate pastime, so much so that Seattleites check out more books per capita than people in any other city. Now with a world-class main library, book lovers can set new records.

Seattle Public Library *(above)*

Seattle's new, 11-story library, with a glass and steel skin of odd-angled pop-outs and crayon-colored, interior walls and escalators, is a bold and crowning achievement for a city of avid readers. Designed by famous Dutch architect Rem Koolhaas, this unpredictable building changes shape with every level, skewing sideways abruptly to take advantage of downtown views. Yet, inside, the dance of form and function makes remarkable sense. Lattes (with covers) are allowed inside. Perfect!

The Space Needle under a Full Moon *(opposite)*

Rising 60 feet above Seattle Center, the city's most recognizable landmark looks like a landing platform for space travelers from the moon. The red-roofed building to its right is home to the SuperSonics, Seattle's NBA team.

Monorail at Seattle Center

(top)

Originally built as futuristic transportation for the 1962 World's Fair, the monorail is still a thrilling 90-second ride for tourists and locals from downtown to the Seattle Center.

Space Needle Entrance, Seattle Center *(bottom)*

A fast elevator is ready to whisk you up 500 feet to a revolving restaurant, or twenty feet higher to the wrap-around, observation deck. Enjoy spectacular views of the city, Puget Sound, Mount Rainier to the south, and mountain ranges east and west.

**Experience Music Project,
Seattle Center** *(above)*

In the shape of a "shattered" guitar, EMP, designed by Frank Gehry, celebrates the creative process of music making with multimedia exhibits and large, concert spaces. Magically, Seattle's two monorail tracks end here and become "guitar strings."

Chief Seattle Statue *(left)*

"There was a time when our people covered the land as the waves of a wind-ruffled sea.... that time has long since passed... I will not mourn..." Spoken by Duwamish Indian Chief Seattle, whose tribe was moved to a reservation in the 1850's.

**"Hammering Man,"
Seattle Art Museum** *(opposite)*

The excitement of this world-class art museum's collections begins outside with a 48-ft "celebration of the worker" by acclaimed artist Jonathan Borofsky. The arm hammers silently four times per minute.

Troll Under Fremont Bridge *(top)*

Seattle's eclectic Fremont district uses public art to show off its serious quirkiness. Hiding under the Fremont Bridge, one of the nation's busiest drawbridges, is a massive troll squashing a real Volkwagen bug, presumably plucked from traffic above!

Fallen Firefighters' Memorial, Pioneer Square *(bottom)*

Created by University of Washington graduate Hai Ying Wu, this life-size, bronze sculpture honors the bravery of Seattle firefighters who have died in the line of duty throughout the fire department's history.

Tlingit Totem Pole, Pioneer Square *(opposite)*

Carved in the 1930's in the distinctive red, black and green colors of the Alaskan Tlingit tribe, the 60-foot totem tells tribal legends of the Raven and Creation, the woman who married a frog, and the raven and mink trapped in a whale's belly.

Jimi Hendrix Statue

This solitary statue celebrates legendary rock guitarist Jimi Hendrix. In the limelight for just four years until his death at 27, this Seattle native's musical virtuosity and style continue to mesmerize his fans.

Bruce Lee and Brandon Lee Graves, Lakeview Cemetery

People come from all over the world to pay respects to the late martial arts great Bruce Lee, a Seattle native. Buried next to him is his son, Brandon, who was killed in a shooting accident while starring in the film, "The Crow."

Museum of Flight *(pages 56 and 57)*

Attracting over 400,000 visitors annually, the Museum of Flight is a special place of pride for The Boeing Company's hometown crowd. The museum encompasses the famous "Red Barn®," Boeing's original manufacturing facility.

The "Great Gallery" (opposite, bottom) is a massive, glass-and-steel exhibit hall that traces the history of the first century of flight. It contains thirty-nine, full-size, historic aircraft, including a nine-ton Douglas DC-3.

The museum is one of the largest air and space museums in the world, with an impressive collection that includes more than 150 historically significant air and spacecraft such as this 1942 Waco UPF-7 Bi-Plane (above).

Scenic Flights over Puget Sound
(above)

Suddenly the year is 1942 in the brilliant, blue skies over Seattle. This vintage Waco UPF-7 is one of seven antique bi-planes that provides thrilling air tours, available through Olde Thyme Aviation, Inc., at the Museum of Flight.

Historic Ship Wharf, South Lake Union Park *(opposite, top)*

The maritime heritage of the Northwest is the focus for this new, 12-acre park on Lake Union, a popular downtown lake. Visitors can hop aboard a classic, wooden sailboat or rowboat any Sunday afternoon, free of charge.

Historic Ship Wharf Workshop, South Lake Union Park *(opposite, bottom)*

There is plenty to do here if you want to combine fun with learning. The park's ambitious program features historic vessels, boat-building classes, boat rentals, sailing classes, family programs and festivals—all ingredients for a great day in Seattle.

Folklife Festival, Seattle Center

This beloved music festival is
Seattle's unofficial leap into summer.
Held every year over Memorial Day
weekend, the four-day gala brings
together 250,000 visitors, and thousands of musicians and volunteers.

Victor Steinbrueck Park

Seattle is a city with wonderful expanses of lush parks and green spaces that provide stunning, scenic views of the city and the surrounding mountains and waterways. Here, people relax and enjoy the warmth of a sunny day at the Victor Steinbrueck Park.

Folklife Festival, Seattle Center

(above and opposite, top)

This free, music festival is a celebration of year-round ethnic, folk, and traditional arts activities. Artists from the Pacific Northwest and special guests from around the world create an ethnic extravaganza embracing music and dance performances, visual arts, and folklore exhibits. The festival's exuberant tradition of sharing and participation encourages exploration and learning between participants and public alike.

"Waiting for the Interurban"

(opposite, bottom)

In the heart of Fremont, Seattle's quirkiest neighborhood, is this playful, life-size sculpture of people waiting to ride the long-gone Interurban Trolley. Neighbors often add streamers, balloons or castoff clothing to Richard Beyer's sculpture.

Log House Museum, Alki Beach

Housed in one of the last original,
turn-of-the-century log homes, this
award-winning museum celebrates
the history and heritage of the Alki
neighborhood, the site of Seattle's
first white settlement in 1851.

International District *(above and right)*

One of Seattle's oldest areas, the Chinatown-International District is the colorful, cultural hub of Seattle's Asian-American community. Wonderful Asian restaurants, shops and historic attractions draw appreciative crowds every day.

Each summer, the International District hosts the largest Pan-Asian-American street fair in the Pacific Northwest, featuring arts and crafts, great food, martial arts shows, dragon dances, Filipino dancing and Japanese Taiko drumming.

**Japanese Garden, Washington
Park Arboretum**

On the shores of Lake Washington,
the Washington Park Arboretum's
spectacular 230 acres lavishly show-
case America's largest collections of
oaks, conifers, camellias, Japanese
maples and hollies.

Great Blue Heron, Washington Park Arboretum

This urban green space is an important fish and wildlife habitat for federally listed species such as Chinook salmon and nesting bald eagles. Visitors enjoy this nature refuge while walking along its shoreline paths or canoeing its waterways.

Lincoln Park, West Seattle

Lincoln Park attracts people year 'round with its salt-water pool, tennis courts, picnic areas, horseshoe pits, and hiking trails into the dense woods overlooking the beach. Above, cyclists pause for a rest at the Colman Pool complex.

Cycling in Lincoln Park *(top)*

There is plenty to do at this popular, 135-acre park in West Seattle. A paved walkway on the beach is a favorite with outdoor enthusiasts who love to walk, jog, rollerblade or cycle, while the waters of Puget Sound gently touch the shore.

Colman Pool, Lincoln Park *(bottom)*

It began as a tide-fed swimming hole in 1929. It became so popular that West Seattle residents began asking for a real pool. In 1941, this heated, salt-water pool opened for business, thanks to Kenneth Colman's $150,000 donation.

Pioneer Square Underground Tour

(opposite, top, bottom)

History is literally beneath your feet in Pioneer Square, the 1851 birthplace of modern Seattle. This unique tour takes you through subterranean passages that once were the main roadways and first-floor storefronts of the old downtown.

Familiar Sights on Puget Sound

(above)

While sailing is a favorite recreation for avid boaters in Seattle, the country's largest ferry system is all business, transporting millions of people and their vehicles safely and punctually from one Puget Sound port to another.

Downtown Seattle and Mt. Rainier from Kerry Park *(previous page)*

This spectacular view says "Seattle" better than any other city view. In the foreground, the treetops of the chic, Queen Anne neighborhood frame the panoramic view of the Space Needle, the city skyline, and, magnificent Mount Rainier.

Skagit Valley Tulip Festival
(above)

Every Spring some half million tourists visit the Skagit Valley to feast their eyes upon the largest harvest of tulips this side of Holland. Hundreds of acres of tulips in wide bands of colors form a vivid rainbow all the way to the horizon.

Skagit Valley Tulip Festival

The Skagit Valley, a fertile area near the coast between Seattle and Vancouver, Canada, dominates the North American tulip industry and is second only to Holland, the world leader. Mother Nature decides exactly when the festival begins. Dainty, yellow daffodils are the first to show their colors in March, followed by a profusion of tulips in April. Irises and lilies follow in rapid succession and provide "ooh's" and "ahhh's" well into the month of May.

Century Center Red Clock *(left)*

Sporting a fresh coat of bright paint, this sidewalk clock was originally built for Zedick Jewelers over fifty years ago. Today it is a landmark at Century Center, a modern complex of shops and an office tower.

Ben Bridge Jewelers Clock *(right)*

This stately clock is the last of the clocks on Pike Street, once the most densely clocked street in Seattle. Street clocks were very important in the early days when the average citizen could not afford a timepiece.

Carroll's Fine Jewelry Clock *(opposite)*

This magnificent clock was built in 1913 by the owner of Carroll's Jewelry. Since then, the 20-ft-tall, two-ton clock has become an historic landmark in Seattle's downtown community.

**Seattle Asian Art Museum,
Volunteer Park** *(above)*

Situated on the edge of a bluff
amidst the lush foliage of Volunteer
Park, this 1933 Art Moderne building houses internationally renowned
collections of sculpture, pottery, and
textiles from China, Japan, India,
Korea, and several Southeast Asian
countries. Much of the artwork was
personally collected by the late
Eugene Fuller, Seattle's most famous
art collector.

Volunteer Park Conservatory

(opposite)

This 1912 Victorian conservatory
showcases an extensive collection of
exotic palms, ferns, bromeliads,
orchids, and cactus amidst grounds
landscaped by the world-famous
Olmstead brothers, designers of
New York's Central Park.

Green Lake Park

Green Lake's refreshing expanse of water and landscape is a welcome sight in the heart of this densely populated neighborhood. The lakeside path is a favorite with walkers, joggers, bikers, and skaters.

Roadside Art on Vashon Island

(above)

For an island of 10,000 people, Vashon offers visitors a surprising number of opportunities to enjoy the arts, including: galleries, shows, arts and crafts exhibits, while a community theater provide year-round events for all ages.

Safeco Field

It didn't take long for Seattle's new baseball park to earn a national reputation. Since their inaugural game in 1999, Seattle's beloved Mariners have played to sold-out crowds eager to experience one of the nation's greatest ballparks. It's always easy to follow the game action with the park's comprehensive scoreboard system and unique play-by-play boards. Safeco Field's downtown location rewards fans with panoramic views of the skyline and Puget Sound.

Outdoor Art on Vashon Island

(top)

Vashon Island is an island with an artistic personality. Its vibrant arts and crafts community decorates the island with whimsical sculptures and other works of art that invite you to stop what you're doing and come play.

Bus Shelter Art, Volunteer Park

(bottom)

Thanks to King County's delightful, bus-shelter art program, waiting for a bus on a rainy day in Seattle can actually be fun. Local artists have created murals using media such as tiles, laser-cut steel and paints.

Alki Beach, West Seattle

One year after white settlers landed on Alki Point in 1851, the group leader abandoned the site for a better location on the east shore of Elliott Bay. Now a part of Seattle's vibrant downtown area, the new site is known as Pioneer Square.

Alki Point, West Seattle

The original twenty-two white settlers of Seattle landed in 1851 on
Alki Point, the southernmost tip of
the entrance to Elliott Bay, Seattle's
harbor. They ambitiously named it
"New York." As time passed, reality
set in about their development as a
major city. More modestly, they
added the Chinook word "Alki"
which means "by and by."
Eventually, as New York-Alki proved
to be no match for its eastern coun-
terpart, Seattle's original settlement
became known simply as Alki.

Tillicum Village Harbor, Blake Island *(above)*

Eight miles from Seattle's downtown waterfront, scenic Blake Island State Park beckons visitors with beautiful campgrounds, nature trails, beaches, and a unique way to experience Northwest Coast Native American culture.

Downtown Seattle Skyline

(opposite)

In a picture-perfect setting on Puget Sound, just 113 miles south of the Canadian border, Seattle has become a commercial, cultural and advanced technology hub of the Pacific Northwest and a major port for trans-Pacific and European trade.

Seattle View from Alki Beach

With great views of Seattle, Alki
Beach is a quirky, California-style
beach town. Its sandy shores, paved
pathway, inexpensive restaurants
and souvenir shops attract a colorful
group of sun worshipers, joggers,
skaters and cyclists.

Alki Point Lighthouse

The Alki Point Lighthouse is one of thirteen along the shores of Puget Sound that helps mariners move safely through this busy, marine traffic area. Built in 1913, the 37-foot octagonal tower is attached to a fog signal building.

Port Townsend, Olympic Peninsula

(above)

Tourists love this delightfully quirky harbor town with its 19th century, hilltop, Victorian mansions and an historic downtown district of brick and stone buildings. Coffee houses, cafés, and art galleries add a distinct, bohemian flair.

Alki Beach Anchor

(opposite, top)

A massive rusty anchor, showcased on Alki Beach, is a dramatic reminder of the heavy, marine traffic of ferries, container ships, barges, and fishing vessels that make Seattle one of the busiest international harbors in the country.

Fishing Fleet in Harbor

(opposite, bottom)

A major player in America's fishing industry, greater Seattle is the home-port to the U.S. North Pacific fishing fleet and is the point of entry for fifty percent of the seafood sold in the United States.

Sailing Puget Sound

The waters of greater Seattle make this special corner of the world a boaters' paradise. One out of every five people own a boat. This twenty-percent statistic means that greater Seattle is home to the country's highest concentration of boaters.

Kayaks on Alki Beach

Alki Beach is a popular launch point for serious kayakers eager to maneuver the four-mile crossing to Blake Island amidst Puget Sound's steady marine traffic. Overnight island lodging includes campgrounds or a traditional Indian longhouse.

Low Tide at Alki Beach Park

In the summer, this West Seattle beach teems with locals and tourists who come to sunbathe, swim, or relax and read a good book amidst breathtaking, panoramic views of Puget Sound, Seattle and the Olympic Mountains.

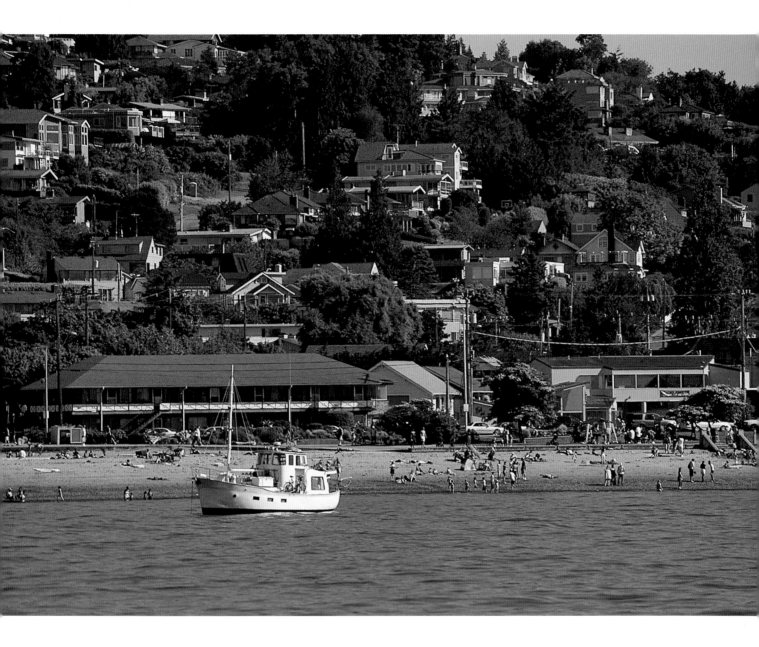

Alki Beach from Ferry

Rising dramatically above the beach, this West Seattle neighborhood is one of the city's most fashionable. Modest bungalows and pricey condos on the beach give way to hillside, high-end homes with priceless, panoramic views.

Seattle Waterfront *(above)*

The giant, orange cranes that hoist containers on and off of railroad cars and ships are a familiar part of the harbor skyline. Together, the Ports of Seattle and Tacoma, 30 miles south, are the second-largest-volume container center in the country.

Zero to "Wow!" in 41 Seconds

(opposite)

The ride to the top of the Space Needle elevates you above the local neighborhood to experience the panoramic setting of this charmed city on the bay. Sparkling lakes, waterways and mountain ranges create a visual feast.

Downtown View from Queen Anne Neighborhood

Even in the late 19th century, Seattle's earliest pioneers knew prime real estate when they saw it and began to lay claim to and subdivide Queen Anne Hill, the highest hill in town at 450 feet above sea level.

Scuba Divers off Alki Beach

The sandy, two-mile stretch of scenic Alki Beach in West Seattle has become a premier, outdoor classroom for scuba instructors. Students experience activities such as wreck diving, underwater photography and marine life identification.

Downtown View from Kerry Park
(previous page)

One look at Seattle's skyline tells you that this Northwest city enjoys living on the architectural edge—from the Space Needle to the Experience Music Project (red and metal shape near flag) with its crouching shape suggesting a broken guitar.

Puget Sound and Olympic Mountains *(above)*

Rising 450 feet above Puget Sound on the highest hill in town, the fashionable Queen Anne neighborhood offers sweeping water and mountain views, just minutes from downtown.

Puget Sound and Olympic Mountains

Seattle's hilly terrain provides breath-taking views from many points around the city. However, from the top of Queen Anne, the views are indisputably the best in the city.

Lake Washington (*above*)

Amidst stunning scenery, Lake Washington's fifty-one-mile, serpentine shoreline is home to many of the most beautiful and expensive houses in the Seattle metro area.

Seattle's Favorite Icon (*opposite*)

Long after the 1962 World's Fair came and went, the Space Needle remains Seattle's #1 attraction. It is part of Seattle Center, a 74-acre cultural and entertainment venue for opera, theater, ballet, science, movies, laser shows and community events.

Tug Boats at Day's End

The bustling ports of greater Seattle
include: Seattle, Tacoma to the south
and Everett to the north. Together,
they utilize the largest number of
working tugboats on the west coast.
The area's flourishing maritime
industry gets bigger every day.

Sunset at Seattle's Waterfront

There is a special purity to a Seattle sunset down on the waterfront, as the last light of day infuses a golden hue on buildings no longer teeming with people and bay waters no longer churning with the comings and goings of boats.

Tugboat Going to Work

It is hard to imagine tugboats, the
backbone of Seattle's busy harbor,
ever having fun. Yet, every spring,
during Maritime Week, these hard-
working boats and their skippers
get to frolic in the sun during the
country's largest tugboat race.

Tugboat Hard at Work

In Seattle's busy, deep-water harbor, colorful tugboats are everywhere, pulling barges, guiding huge steamers and container ships in and out of the bay, and bringing disabled boats in for dock-side repairs.

Vashon Island Ferry Dock

There is always something magical about an island that can only be reached by boat. Vashon Island is a short, ferry ride from Seattle and offers breathtaking views of the city, the Olympic and Cascade Mountains, and Mt. Rainier.

Lake Washington Boat Harbor

The second largest lake in the state, Lake Washington is a boater's paradise. With many small coves and inlets, the shoreline has over 900 recreational docks and over 500 marina docks to help people get out on the water fast!

Lincoln Park

With a pristine, mile-long shoreline
curving along picturesque Puget
Sound, this West Seattle park is one
of Seattle's largest and most popular
public spaces for swimming, pic-
nicking, walking and cycling.

Microsoft Campus, Redmond

This is corporate headquarters of the little software company started by Bill Gates and Paul Allen in 1975. Their bold vision of seeing "a PC on every desk and in every home" was realized beyond their wildest dreams. From its beautifully land-scaped campus thirteen miles from Seattle, the Fortune 500 giant man-ages an international staff of 50,000 employees, 22,000 of whom are on the Redmond campus.

Searching for Sixgills, Seattle Aquarium

Important shark research is conducted right under the piers of the aquarium. Visitors can watch actual video footage of research in action with "Sixgills," the third largest, predatory shark in the world.

Seattle Aquarium *(top)*

This award-winning aquarium features a spectacular "Underwater Dome." A short tunnel leads visitors into a spherical undersea room with 360-degree views of Pacific Northwest fish such as sharks, salmon, ling cod, sturgeon and halibut.

Tidal Pool, Seattle Aquarium *(bottom)*

The aquarium's "Life on the Edge" exhibit shows visitors the unique lifestyles of the amazing sea creatures that survive and thrive in the harsh conditions of Washington's outer coast and inland sea tidal zones.

**"Dance on the Wind" Show,
Tillicum Village** *(above)*

Tillicum Village on Blake Island
helps visitors experience the unique
culture and traditions of the
Northwest Coast Indians, complete
with a salmon bake in an authentic,
cedar longhouse and a spellbinding
interpretative dance finale.

Tillicum Village Totem Pole

(opposite)

Totem poles are a unique expression
of Northwest Native American
culture and tell much about their
beliefs and legends. Visitors to Tillicum Village enjoy watching native
artisans in the process of carving
totem poles out of cedar logs.

Woodland Park Zoo Entrance Gate Sculpture

Animals sit on top of the world at the entrance to the zoo, a fitting sculpture for the organization's internationally recognized conservation programs.

Woodland Park Zoo Butterflies & Blooms Exhibit *(top)*

The four stages of a butterfly's life are showcased in real life at this popular exhibit. Visitors witness hundreds of vibrant butterflies emerge from their chrysalis and begin flying for the first time in various butterfly surroundings.

Woodland Park Zoo Entrance Gates *(bottom)*

Many of the 300 species in this 92-acre botanical garden roam freely in award-winning habitat areas that focus on ecosystems rather than single species: example, the Alaska habitat is home to Kodiak bears that catch live trout out of a stream.

**Elephant Forest Exhibit, Woodland
Park Zoo**

Zoo visitors love to watch the
African and smaller Asian elephants
bathe and spray themselves. Their
massive trunks hold over two gallons of water and are so dexterous
that they can pick up a single grain
of rice.

Patas Monkey, Woodland Park Zoo

Monkeys are always fun to watch, but these ground-dwelling Patas will really make you smile. Just like humans, they like to relax by leaning back and putting up their feet!

**Canada Goose, Olympic National
Park** *(above and opposite)*

With almost one million acres of
primeval landscape, Olympic
National Park is one of the largest
wildlife breeding grounds in the
Pacific Northwest. Avid bird watch-
ers call this special place "paradise."

The top of a fallen tree provides a
perfect perch for a nesting Canada
goose, one of millions of migrating
waterfowl and birds who make this
special stop on their way across the
Pacific Flyway.

Olympic National Park, Olympic Peninsula *(above and opposite)*

Across Puget Sound from Seattle, the massive Olympic Peninsula is a natural wonderland. On its west coast, the cool waters of the Pacific Ocean lap against the shores of fog-shrouded beaches. Inland are the only rainforests in the contiguous United States, where living plants flourish on almost every square inch of space, from towering Sitka spruces to lush ferns and mosses. The park also encompasses pristine alpine and sub-alpine scenery laced with lush meadows and mountain streams.

Mt. Rainier National Park, Nickel Creek *(above)*

Cold creek waters rush over a rocky bed on Mt. Rainier's popular Wonderland Trail. Just one mile from the trail head, the creek gives hikers comfortable campsites on the way up this mystical, towering mountain.

Olympic National Park, Sol Duc Falls *(opposite)*

A short hike through an old forest of giant hemlocks and Douglas firs rewards visitors with Sol Duc Falls, one of the largest and most stunning waterfalls in the park, dramatically viewed from a bridge that crosses the canyon just below the falls.

photo: by Brad Perks

Roger L. Johnson Photography

A professional photographer for over 30 years, Roger L. Johnson's work has taken him to all seven continents of the globe. In 1995, Johnson achieved worldwide recognition for his nature studies when he won first place in the prestigious *Wildlife Photographer of the Year* competition sponsored by the Natural History Museum, in London, England. He has been awarded "Best of Show" in numerous state and local competitions. His photos have been published in Japan, England, and throughout the United States and Europe.

A former owner of a custom color lab and commercial photography studio, Johnson has a strong understanding of the photographic publication industry. He is a past president and an active member of the *Contra Costa Camera Club*, a participant in numerous PSA Salons, and a respected judge for a variety of photographic events in California.

A graduate of Brooks Institute of Photography in Santa Barbara, California, the artist finds great personal satisfaction in sharing the way that he sees the world through his camera lens. To view more of Johnson's world, visit his web site at www.rljphoto.com.